The Gamut

a memoir

Helen Reed

The Gamut

a memoir

© 2010 Helen Reed
ISBN 978-0-9661378-1-1

Editing: Cathy Kline
Book Design and Production: Barbara With

Synergy Alliance, a division of
Mad Island Communications
P.O. Box 153
La Pointe, WI 54850
barbarawith11@aol.com
www.barbarawith.com

Acknowledgments

For all of my family and friends, especially Jeannette McDonald who started the ball rolling and Cathy Kline who helped me make it a reality.

Table of Contents

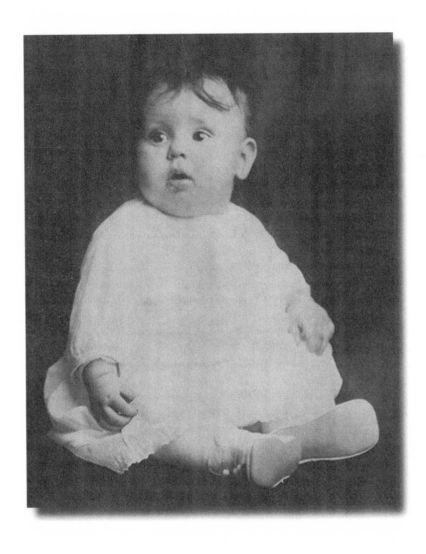

Introduction

I am the same age as Betty White, one of the *Golden Girls*. She is still going strong, making movies, winning awards and being interviewed on TV. Recently, Betty received her 5th prime time Emmy and is starting another television series. Both of us are keeping busy, achieving goals and fulfilling dreams.

My place of birth was Youngstown, Ohio in 1922 with the help of a midwife on Federal Street. In those days, babies were delivered at home. My sister, Mary, was born in 1920, my brother, Joe, was born 1924. He died August 21, 2000. Another boy, named Alex, was born before Mary, but only lived for six months. In those days, it was common for first born babies to die—so I was told—perhaps, because of difficult births. When Mary lost her first child, she was told it's not that unusual.

Well, not me. My first child, Gayle, did not follow that pattern. Perhaps at the time, due to my being an unwed mother, they did not expect her to live. Although that was not the case, as she was a healthy, happy baby.

My dad, Alex Orosz, was born in Hungary in 1895. His mother died in childbirth and he was raised by his grandmother. His father came to the United States before WWI, settling in Louisiana. Dad was in college when the war started and his grandmother sent him to the US so that he wouldn't have to go to war. He was an illegal alien and never went back. Dad's name in Hungarian is Orosz Sandor. He was an only child. I can only imagine how heartbreaking it was for his grandmother to give him up.

Mom was born in Hammond, Louisiana in 1900. There were four sisters in the Maklary family: Emma, Mary, Helen (mom) and Vera. Since grandpa always wanted sons, he blamed grandma for having girls. As a result, grandma had a nervous breakdown while Mom was very young. Grandma was put in an institution where she spent the rest of her life. Mom had a nervous breakdown when I was eight years old, but dad kept her home. Due to financial set-backs, our family moved into an upstairs apartment. An old couple lived downstairs and continually complained about the noise we made.

Finally Mom's sister Vera came from Chicago, found a house with a big yard and we moved to 518 Steel Street on the streetcar line.

Later, mom and Aunt Vera went by bus to Highlands, Texas for about a month, where the other two sisters lived. That left me and dad in charge. My sister, Mary, was always sickly, so she was not much help and since Joe was the baby, nothing was expected of him. I went to the store, carried home groceries and dad cooked. He did the washing in the Maytag washer in the basement and I hung out the clothes. He'd scrub the floor. I would do the dishes.

During the years that followed the four sisters would go to Louisiana to visit their mom at the institution where she lived her life in peace. The four girls had been raised by a stepmother who made them work in the strawberry fields. They went to school only rarely. Mom got as far as the third grade.

Grandpa married off three of the daughters by the time they were 16 and Vera, the youngest, left home. He sold the farm and bought another in Kentucky. Later he moved to upstate New York where he farmed with his sister Sophie. Before WWII, he went back to Hungary to live with his brothers. Grandpa died there.

During WWII, I took a bus trip to Los Angeles, California to visit Aunt Vera, her husband John and their five-year-old son, Frankie. Several years later I visited my cousins in Texas. Aunt Emma had eight children and Aunt Mary had one son who grew up with his eight cousins. Aunt Mary floated around and married two or three times.

I never knew any of my grandparents. Mom and dad returned to Louisiana shortly after I was born but had to come back to Youngstown. Dad could not live in Louisiana as he had contracted malaria there and was now susceptible.

Our next home was a two room double at 1610 Manhattan Avenue. We needed more space and moved to a larger house at 1649 Manhattan. It was a two story with a basement and a huge yard. Mom got over her homesickness here. When the stock market crashed and the steel mills shut down, we had to move again. The next move to Maryland Avenue was where mom threw in the towel. I became very capable doing whatever had to be done, while mom stayed in bed and cried.

School was one block away and I looked forward to it. Learning was easy for me. I always got good grades. The teachers liked me. School was fun—an escape from the dreariness at home.

When we moved to Steel Street, dad worked one day a week as the mills operated on a small scale. The men would congregate on our front porch and play cards. Sometimes they would have a cookout in the back yard. They'd make a fire, roast bacon on a stick and drip the grease over hunks of rye bread.

I loved the smell of fresh bread and goodies from the bakery across the street. We would buy bread shortly after it came out of the oven. Bread had chewy crusts—good for the teeth.

Again, another change. Finally, a house of our own—no more rentals! I was out of high school and working part time. I encouraged dad to purchase, we signed the contract and the house on 110 South Osborn Street was built. Just before the plumbing was installed, war broke out. That was my last Youngstown address.

1 The Early Years

This is the beginning of a long planned story. I've never talked about writing my memoirs but have given it a lot of thought. My friend, Betty, urged me to write a book since I've had so many various adventures. She even suggested the title "The Gamut"...so here goes.

I grew up during the Great Depression. I never felt deprived. We always had enough to eat and a roof over our heads. Occasionally I'd get something new, but mostly wore hand-me-downs. Everyone did it. Clothes were passed around. Since I was a tomboy I wore out shoes fast. Dad would buy leather or rubber heels and resole my shoes and hammer on new heels as needed. My sister was very delicate and never wore out her shoes. I did that. To this day she is still dainty and wears high heels. I gave up the heels after I retired. Flats do the job for me.

I attribute my good health to my upbringing. We never had junk food in our house and always ate home cooked meals. "An apple a day keeps the doctor away" was conscientiously followed. We were never out of apples and had other fruits in season.

We always had a big garden and lots of fresh vegetables. Mom would can everything in Mason jars. My job was to wash everything. Everyone worked in the garden weeding and watering among other things. I guess that's why I've never had a garden since I left home. I am "gardened" out. I even have trouble keeping a plant alive. They must sense my dislike of those care-taking chores. I do have one plant that has survived over twenty years. It thrives on being ignored, being a member of the cactus family – an *aloe*. This type of plant requires very little water. Sometimes I'm gone for several weeks at a time, but it refuses to give up.

Dad had money saved that he couldn't get, so he ran a grocery bill. (Later when the banks reopened he was able to pay off the debt.) He would go to market on the streetcar and bring home baskets of fruits and vegetables to be canned. More jars to be washed! We never bought any groceries in cans. Chickens were bought alive and mom killed and dressed them. We never bought hamburger. If meat had to be ground, it was done by hand on our grinder. We didn't eat meat everyday of the week. We ate all kinds of home cooked soups. We always drank milk. As kids we were allowed to drink coffee with boiled milk and sugar. To this day I still like my coffee with milk (not boiled) and sugar.

There were soup kitchens and milk lines. We never went to the soup kitchen, but we were first in line with our gallon jugs for milk. Our house was next to a vacant building where they set up to sell the milk. Twice a week a line formed around the block. Milk was four cents a gallon.

This was an ethnic neighborhood where parents rarely spoke English. We knew common words in several languages. I had trouble with English when I started school, as we only spoke Hungarian at home. Dad came from Hungary and mom's parents also.

Mom grew up in Hammond, Louisiana where they had a strawberry farm. It's a Hungarian community to this day. One of my grandparents is buried in a Catholic cemetery, another in the Protestant one across the road.

Dad was the Catholic parent. He went to church with us every Sunday. Mom didn't go. She had different views. We heard them growing up. By the time I was twelve years old I knew I would not be a Catholic. I hated to listen to sermons about burning in Hell for sins committed. I was a good kid, never did anything really wrong.

However, kids were seen and not heard. You kept your opinions to yourself. I adored my father and continued to go to church until I left home. To me, church was a social event. They held banquets, picnics and dances where families of all ages got together. It was a fun thing.

As the years went by I attended different churches: Baptist, Lutheran, Methodist and others. I finally decided to become a Methodist. I became a member and took my three children, Gayle, Joyce and Don to church every Sunday. Joyce, at the age of four, volunteered me for her Sunday school teacher when the position opened. I taught for ten years at both the Third Avenue Methodist on High Street and the McKendree Methodist Church on Cleveland Avenue.

Though money was scarce we had the necessary toys such as roller skates, wagons, sleds and ice skates. In the summer we also jumped rope and played hopscotch. We'd have ball games and dad would watch. We walked everywhere. The streetcar ran in front of our house, mostly empty. On rare occasions, we would ride it on Sunday to church down Mahoning Avenue. Mostly, though, we'd walk the shorter way on the railroad track, a different route where few trains passed.

Chaney High school was two miles away and we walked five days a week even in the dead of winter through snow and zero temperatures. "Snow days" were non-existent. This was healthy living! We spent a lot of time outdoors. In addition, indoor exercise consisted of scrubbing floors on your knees along with other chores. Mom would stand watching over to advise me. To this day I dislike housework.

For entertainment, friends would sit on the front porch and we'd sing and chat. If we had to be inside, we would play cards or shoot marbles on the floor. We did get a radio and we had a Victrola with many records. When I was 15, we got a phone. The Semko family in our neighborhood owned a car. They lived across the street and the older brother took the car out sometimes. It was a special event when he would take us all for a ride.

There was a flush toilet in the basement. We had a coal stove in the kitchen where we heated water for taking baths in an aluminum tub. We slept in two beds, one for mom and dad and one for three kids. There was no heat in the bedrooms, so to keep us warm, mom made goose-down, feather-tick comforters. I remember mom pulling the feathers off the quills by hand to stuff into the unbleached muslin material. The bed cover was called a *dunya*.

Most days we walked to school with Margaret and Agnes from our neighborhood. We'd walk to the playground on Salts Spring Road where there were swings and a huge sliding board. They held classes in embroidery which I attended. I completed a few small items. A public pool was less than a mile away where it cost five cents to get in. The price of a good car was about $600–gas cost eleven cents a gallon. For a nickel you could buy a bottle of pop, an ice cream cone with two scoops, or ride on the street car. Postage stamps cost three cents and it only took a penny to send a postcard.

Televisions, dishwashers and air conditioners had not yet been invented. Ice was delivered in 25 or 50 pound chunks. A pan under the ice box had to be emptied regularly as the ice melted. The "rag man" had a horse pulling a wagon collecting junk. The 5 &10 cent store sold items that were five and ten cents. Hardware was a store, not the opposite of software. Of course, there were no computers, no plastic, but something similar called cellophane. Nylon hose were introduced just before the war and panty hose years later. There was no McDonald's and no instant coffee. Cigarette smoking was glamorous, grass was what you mowed and pot was what you used for cooking. Movies cost five cents. Dad would go with us on Saturday afternoon to the theater on Mahoning Avenue where we saw a lot of westerns with Gene Autry and Roy Rogers. We loved their songs such as "Back in the Saddle Again."

During the summer we went to picnics where complete families, young and old alike, danced to live music. Every August, Hungarian Day at Idora Park was a special event where old friends and neighbors reunited. Live orchestras played for those who wanted to dance. There were rides for all ages. I liked the Wildcat Roller Coaster going very fast up and down hills. Each ride was only a few pennies. We went to Polish Day where everyone danced the polka. Programs were in native language and dress. The Hungarians danced the "czardas" in their country colors of red, white and green.

As teenagers, my sister and I rode the streetcar to go ballroom dancing at various dance halls. My favorite was the Elms Ballroom on the North end of town where they always had a live band. We lived on the West side. I learned to jitterbug in high school from two boys who were gay. They were such good dancers! The big bands came to Youngstown, also. We danced on crowded dance floors to the Dorsey's, Sammy Kaye, Glenn Miller, Artie Shaw and many others.

When Frank Sinatra came to the Palace Theater, the line formed for blocks. We got there early and waited to get in. Everyone loved Frank. Mary and I double-dated. Some of the guys were young men from the Mafia families. They had the big cars and money. They were also good dancers. They treated us royally and expected nothing in return.

I got my first job at a dry goods store two doors away, owned by Mr. Krauss. He also owned several houses including ours. I'd go in to work after school and on Saturdays. My pay was fifty cents a week, which I turned over to my parents. There were few customers. No one had much money. Krauss would carry the accounts and every payday customers would come in and pay something. My sister, Mary, and I took turns working.

One day while Mary was working, a man came in and told her to open the register. She did and he took the money. For a while after the robbery she was a wreck, but eventually she got over it.

Krauss liked women. Sometimes he'd chase me all around the store for a feel, but mostly I was able to escape. Mom was their housekeeper. She'd cook and clean. Every once in awhile he would corner her, too. His wife had her own bakery business so she was rarely at the store. The two sons, Marvin and Robert Krauss, were never at the store when we were working.

My brother, Joe, would go to the city dump, a few blocks away and pick up copper and other stuff which he sold. He got a paper route and delivered the "Vindicator." If there was something important happening they'd put out an "extra" – it cost three cents. Joe would carry them around yelling "extra!"

I helped with the weekly collections. Most customers paid by the week. I knew all the people on his route. The money I collected had to be turned over to my brother and I never got a cut. Boys and girls were treated differently. For my sister and me, money was doled out as needed, but Joe got to keep his. He always had spending money.

When there was a contest for new customers, Joe always did well. He was awarded trips to various big cities such as Washington DC and New York. He always came home with souvenirs from the hotels such as ash trays and towels. On one train trip, Joe brought home a bedspread with "B & O" on it.

Joe bought his first two-wheel bike. I learned to ride it after many attempts. My best friend was Susie Suhy who lived on Butler Avenue. We'd go riding together. The farthest trip was to Milton Dam about eighteen miles away. Susie was an artist and later became a designer. To this day she designs and sews clothes for the elite. Through the years I would visit her, when I drove to Youngstown to see my family. Susie's parents came from Russia. She had two brothers who were also artistic. They were members of the Butler Art Gallery.

Other close friends were Jimmy, Joe and Mary Fuese. They lived across from Washington School on Portland Avenue, where we all attended school. Joe and I were in the same grade. During the war he became a Marine paratrooper. After a medical discharge, Joe had a career with the Federal government. Back in grade school, Margaret, the friend I used to walk to school with, had a crush on Joe. I've seen him off and on through the years. Recently Joe called to tell me that he married

Margaret. She and Joe had both been widowed and now live in Virginia.

From seventh grade at Washington School, we went to Chaney High on Hazelwood Avenue. My biggest achievement in grade school was seventh grade spelling champion. At Chaney High we got schedules and started changing classes. Here we met new friends. They came from various other schools. History was my favorite subject. Maybe it's because dad liked to talk about it. My sister and brother were never interested. I listened and asked questions. He was so proud of me! I was always on the honor roll. School was easy for me and I loved to read. Not so with the other two, they struggled.

There was no kindergarten when I started school. I'm a born southpaw. Early on I did everything left handed. At the table I was not permitted to eat with my left hand, so I adapted to using my right one but never could cut meat with it. In the first and second grades, I was forced to use my right hand. I was so confused I didn't know forward from backward. I'd turn in papers, which on one side I'd write from left to right and on the other side from right to left. To this day I have no trouble reading or writing backward or upside down. Finally, in third grade I was allowed to do it my way. Remember, Einstein was left-handed. I started wearing a ring on my left hand so I'd know which was which. To this day I wear a ring on my left hand to keep from getting confused. When driving and there's a left turn, I reach for the ring. I've learned to live with it.

My favorite high school teacher was E.J. Miller. He taught a speech class. We went to other schools for declamation contests and debates. Some parents helped by providing transportation. I took a drama class and performed in a couple of school plays. I was elected to the National Honor Society, nominated and elected Secretary of my graduating class of January 1940. I placed second, therefore, no scholarship for me.

I worked part-time and attended Youngstown College for a while. Mom went to Texas again and I had to take over household chores. I dropped out of college. It was either that or give up my social life. I liked to dance and go on dates. Through the years I have attended various colleges and universities, and accumulated credit hours. I don't know if I'll ever get a degree, but it's no longer on my list of things to do.

When World War II started, many changes took place for the war effort. Manufacturing of cars ceased, as all steel went into making tanks, ammunitions and other necessities of war. Isaly Dairy bought horses and wagons for milk delivery. The dairy hired me for one of the home delivery routes. Women replaced men in factories where they manned assembly lines turning out parts for tanks, ships and planes. Shortages mounted and rationing began. Coupons were issued for sugar, gas and shoes. Nylon hose were not available as all nylon went into parachutes. Friends and families of the volunteers and draftees gathered at the train depot to see the boys off to war on crowded trains to various military destinations. Letter writing increased on a large scale.

I became an air raid warden and was issued a gas mask. The war effort united everyone as we contributed time and money for a successful outcome of the war.

2 After High School - World War II

Jobs were scarce when I graduated. I was glad to have a part-time job as a clerk at Woolworth's downtown on Federal Street. I was in the hosiery department and eventually became a buyer. I bought the first order of nylon hose. They had just come out. Working full-time I earned $13.00 a week. We weren't open on Sundays.

I encouraged my dad to buy a house. The steel mills were now on full-time...thanks to Roosevelt's recovery program. They passed the NRA (National Recovery Act). Jobs were becoming more plentiful. Cars were being manufactured. Boys were going to the CCC (Civilian Conservation Camps) where they worked in the national and state parks building roads and structures that still stand today.

That summer in 1940, dad signed a contract to have a house built. It cost $5000. Mary was a secretary and we both handed over our pay checks. We'd be given some spending money. Mom worked cleaning an office downtown. The house was almost completed just before the war broke out December 1941. Only the plumbing had to be put in, but copper was not available. It went into the war effort. The plumbing had to be put in with lead pipes. We moved to 110 South Osborne the following spring. Mom arranged to be gone on a trip, and with the help of friends, we moved in without her help. It was just as well because she was so fussy.

It was wonderful to be in our own house. We had a garage built and later had a black top driveway put in. Dad later retired and lived there till he died. Mom lived there until she went to a nursing home in her 80s. She died at the age of 93. Joe sold the house for $30,000. He gave Mary and me each $300. Though he contributed nothing to having it

built. He figured the money was his since he
had looked after Mom all the years after dad
died. Mary and I had both moved out of town.
Joe and his wife Helen had no children. They
wanted children but were unsuccessful. Mary
had two: Tyra Lea and George. I had three
children: Gayle, Joyce and Don.

Most of the boys I went to school with were
drafted. The President of our class was an early
casualty. My brother, Joe, was classified 4F
because he had varicose veins and flunked the
physical. Mom was so glad he didn't have to
go to war. When I was twenty I wanted to join
the WACs (Women's Army Corps). I needed
parent's signatures, but they would not sign. I
couldn't enlist.

My first war time job was in the Truscon
Steel Mill welding tank treads on an assembly
line. I worked the night shift. They were paying
big money and women were flocking to these
jobs. I hated my job. After about a month they
had a meeting. They had over-hired.

They asked, "Who wants to leave?"

I was the first one out of there. I was relieved to be able to go. When you were hired, you agreed to stay on for the duration of the war. What a break! Mom was upset that I gave up such a good paying job.

The next morning I saw a horse pulling the milk wagon. A young lady dressed in white was delivering milk.

"Mom, you didn't tell me you had a milk maid." I exclaimed.

I ran outside to talk with her. Her name was Virginia. She'd only been working a couple of weeks. They were hiring women and putting on more wagons, as trucks were not available. During the war, no new cars or trucks were manufactured for civilian use.

"Come on down," she said.

"But I don't know how to drive a horse!" I replied.

She said, "There's nothing to it."

I liked horses and could ride.

Mr. Richstone, at the Isaly Dairy Company, interviewed me and I was hired. I picked up the horse and empty wagon on Mahoning Avenue and rode over the bridge to the dairy. I had trouble backing the horse into the loading platform. Chet Reed, who drove a truck on the wholesale route, jumped down and showed me how to do it. Then he helped me load the crates of milk. My supervisor went with me for a couple of days and then I was on my own. Like Virginia said, there was nothing to it.

The horse's name was Joe. He knew all the stops. We were a big attraction. Kids along the route wanted to pet my horse. I was invited into homes for coffee. What a fun job! I loved it! I'd deliver quarts of milk and picked up the empty bottles. Once a month I'd collect. On collection days I had to put a feed bag on Joe and give him water as it took longer. Then back to the dairy to unload the empties and turn in the money. I dated a couple of the guys, but the most interesting one was Chet. One thing led to another and he became the love of my life.

As the men started to return from war, they went back to their jobs and replaced the women. My next job was pumping gas. Chet and I bought a Shell Gas station on 5th Avenue. He continued with the dairy and would come over when he was finished on the wholesale route. We hired a mechanic. I did the book work and collected the ration coupons. This was 1944 and gas was still rationed. After the peace treaties were signed, Chet and I sold the gas station and headed west.

We were on a waiting list to get a new car. The automotive industry was cranking them out and before too long our name came up. We got a red convertible Hudson and headed for Route 66 in January of 1946. We drove through Indiana, Illinois, Missouri, Kansas,

Oklahoma, Texas, New Mexico, Arizona, and California. We had a tent, a kerosene heater along with clothes and necessary items. The top was put down as soon as we hit the warmer climates. We'd go out of our way to see whatever looked interesting. We were free souls with no schedule, no job, just adventure ahead.

When we got to Arizona, we bought a dog. A Great Dane! I was actually afraid of him as we never owned a dog. He sat up front in our one seat convertible leaning on me. We became good friends. We pitched the tent outside Tucson, Arizona and the dog would do guard duty on our day and evening trips. We crossed the border into Nogales, Mexico. I still have the blanket we bought there among other things.

During the war years, Chet was drafted into the Navy and went to Great Lakes Naval Station outside of Chicago. During basic training his knee gave out while he was on guard duty. This was punishment for writing letters when he was suppose to be doing other things.

Since Chet had been a musician, he was offered a place in the Navy but he turned it down. In the meantime he was a typist doing office work. Chet wrote to me every day and some days there were several letters. He wanted me to meet him when he got out. When his unit shipped out, they gave him a medical discharge. I took the train to Chicago.

For one whole week we stayed at the best hotels and went dancing every night to the big bands. Some of the places I remember are the Blackhawk Hotel and Aragon Ballroom. We ate at all the best places in the loop. Then we flew home—my first plane ride!

3   My Love Life

Chet's induction notice was dated December 30, 1943. By this time, having a family did not exempt anyone from the draft. He was ordered to report to Lisbon, Ohio at the Firestone Bank Building at 7:45 a.m. on January 12, 1944. He was sworn in and thirty-two days later got a medical discharge on February 12th.

During this short time he wrote me sixty-six letters and fifteen postcards. Servicemen's mail did not require a stamp. In the upper right hand corner of the envelope or card he would print FREE. Chet wrote interesting letters. He also composed poems about his love for me. On some of the envelopes he printed my name with great flourish. This was done in pencil, before ballpoint pens were invented.

A recent article in the Columbus Dispatch about Hillary Clinton's book, quotes her description of the ex-president as "…still the most interesting, energizing and fully alive person I've ever met." This parallels my feelings about Chet. Later womanizing became another trait, but for a few years he was true to me. Nevertheless, he kept returning. It became an on and off affair.

Hillary grew up a Methodist. I later became one. A saying by John Wesley is mentioned in her book. I had it framed and this quote hung in my bedroom while the kids were growing up. It goes, "Do all the good you can, to all the people you can, as long as you ever can." I always liked that and try to follow it still today.

I guess I should mention some of the things about Chet that caused a lot of grief for me. At the time we met, I did not know he had been married. It all started when Isaly Dairy had a picnic. We played baseball. Chet was on the opposing team. I caught his fly ball and he was out. That so impressed him that he asked me for a date. One thing led to another and we were seeing each other every day. We'd spend hours talking after work. He was never dull.

We started attending sporting events such as boxing matches, baseball games in Cleveland and many diverse activities that I had never been exposed to. He loved football, had played in high school and later as a professional. Chet loved music and was a good dancer. He played the piano and saxophone. During the summer months he played with Sammy Kaye's band in White Sulphur Springs, West Virginia. He married his high school sweetheart Vivian. Four children later he applied for a divorce.

After we'd been dating a few months he told me about Vivian. She was a beautiful woman. They all grew up in East Palestine, Ohio about twenty miles south of Youngstown. Chet had many aunts and uncles. His father, Clyde, was the oldest of nine children. He had eight sisters whom he helped to raise. Clyde chewed tobacco and lived to be 92. Chet's mother, Carrie, had brothers and sisters. Carrie died at the age of 88. She never liked me. She attributed the breakup of his first marriage to me, but that wasn't the way it happened.

I have the article listing his divorce. He did not know it was never finalized until he was in the Navy. When Vivian found out he was dating me she refused to sign the papers. We had planned to get married when Chet was discharged from the Navy. It did not happen. Vivian started calling my mother complaining about how I'd broken up the marriage. Mom got an unlisted number to end the calls. Mom's desire for me to end the relationship with Chet put such a strain on my living with mom, I moved into a house trailer on a farm, where Chet visited me regularly.

We were spending a lot of time together. I became pregnant. Chet wanted me to have an abortion. He even had an address in Akron, Ohio where I could have it done. I refused. When my pregnancy became obvious I decided to leave town. I took a Greyhound bus to Columbus and rented a room at 850 East Broad Street. That building now has law offices. The landlady had her daughter-in-law and granddaughter living there among other residents. We all became good friends.

When my water broke, I took a taxi to the hospital alone. After eight hours in labor, my daughter, Gayle, was born weighing six and one-half pounds. She was a beautiful baby! I had stitches and was pretty sore.

The doctor suspected that I was an unwed mother and urged me to call my mom. Even though we had not spoken in several months, when I called her, she came down and stayed to help me for awhile. I started using Reed as my last name and never talked about my situation.

I got a job at the Bureau of Unemployment
Compensation. I had my name changed to
Reed legally. Gayle and I would take the bus
to Youngstown every now and then. Everyone
loved her. She had blond curly hair and the
sweetest disposition.

I moved in with a family in Worthington
who babysat Gayle while I was at work. They
loved her and wanted to adopt her away from
me. When I realized what was going on, I
moved without leaving a forwarding address.

No one knew where I was, except my
employer. I moved to Clintonville with the
King family. I worked with Ann King who
arranged for her mother-in-law to babysit.
We became great friends, doing a lot together,
going places and playing cards. We stayed up
late—had such fun!

Helen Murray worked with us. She and
I started the same day at the Bureau. Her
husband, Gil, was doing an apprenticeship

as an electrician. They were from Kingston, Tennessee and had no children. She asked if I'd like to live alone. They were renting a house in the country on Lockbourne Road by a small lake. There was an empty boxcar nearby that could be made livable. I could ride to work with them and drop Gayle off at a nursery.

In March we moved into the boxcar. I acquired the basic necessities such as a bed, table and chairs, a few dishes, pans and a hot plate. Finally I was on my own and loved it. I stayed there for a wonderful summer. Helen sewed things for Gayle and we shopped together. By the end of summer, I was able to buy a trailer of my own.

My next address was at a trailer park on Hudson Street. Another girl in the office, Cecelia Ryan, lived there. We rode the bus to the nursery and another bus to work... four buses daily. Gayle had good care at the Northside Day Nursery and played with other children.

It was time to get in touch with my family. Mom had been so nasty I didn't feel like I ever wanted to see her again, but I loved my dad. He did not bitch at me. For two years no one knew of my whereabouts. I took the Greyhound to Youngstown and everyone welcomed me. That ended the feud.

The winter of 1950 was severe, lots of snow and ice. I went home for Thanksgiving and we got snowed in. Ohio State played their football game in the snow. Cars could not drive down Osborn Street. Men got out and shoveled the street. Buses were not running. I was stuck. I had to get back to work. I was finally able to take the train to Columbus. Gayle had to stay with her grandparents and Uncle Joe. They were so happy to do this. Everyone loved her. While I was gone they bought her everything. Dad pulled her on the sled up the hill. Mom took Gayle shopping for pretty dresses and whatever she wanted. This was the beginning of many visits for holidays and other occasions.

I'd let them keep Gayle for up to two weeks at a time.

Chet started to come around and two years later I was pregnant again. Once more I had to relocate. This time I chose Denver, Colorado. Gayle and I rode the train. Through a rental agency I found a basement apartment. The Anderson's at 645 University Boulevard were lovely people. They had a granddaughter Gayle's age. The two would play and go to Sunday school together. They had another daughter in high school. She was dyslexic. I read books for her and helped with her reports.

Again I had a family with whom to be involved. I got a job with the Crane Company in the bookkeeping department. I worked until two weeks before Joyce was born. I was out of touch with everyone back East. I didn't need their lectures. I felt that if I was meant to have babies, there would be a way for me to handle it. My life was my own to live as I chose to. If I made mistakes, they were mine. Everyone makes mistakes. I always had a positive outlook. My needs were taken care of—things just fell into place.

When Joyce's due date was near, I fell down a flight of stairs. My doctor checked me and told me to go to the hospital. He would be going out of town and felt my best bet was to go into forced labor. After I got home I discussed it with Mrs. Anderson. By now, I had lost my nerve.

I called the doctor to tell him I changed my mind and, "I'd wait."

He said, "Get over there right now!" and hung up.

Joyce was born one day short of four years after Gayle in 1952.

When I told Gayle she'd be getting either a baby brother or sister, she said she wanted a sister.

As it happened I had a girl. She was so happy!

Gayle said, "I told you I'd get a baby sister."

I had told everyone I was divorced. There was no mail and no phone calls. A year later Chet got in touch with me. He said I should write to my parents. I was now employed and took a week off. With the two kids I got on a train to Youngstown. Everyone was glad to see us. We had an enjoyable vacation. After another year, I decided to move back to Columbus. I rented an apartment and found a job.

Chet was hauling septic tanks from East Palestine, Ohio to West Virginia to see his customers. Since he was self employed, he was able to stop and visit with us on his way and again on his return.

We left the apartment to move into a half double on Hunter Avenue. When Chet stopped to visit, he'd bring groceries and spend time with his two daughters. Early on Joyce exhibited a temper and cried a lot. He knew how to handle her, as her temperament was similar to his. She was the exact opposite of Gayle. Nevertheless, we all loved her.

Gayle would push her sister in the stroller and had a lovely way of soothing her. Joyce was more difficult when Gayle wasn't around. She would hold her breath to get what she wanted. I'd be terrified. Chet told me to let Joyce pass out, and then she would stop doing it. It was very difficult, but I followed through with his advice and it worked. She never held her breath again.

My babysitter for this phase of our lives was Thelma Kuhn. She lived down the street with her husband and four children. Thelma was very helpful in many ways through the later years. We would keep in touch and do things together. Thelma had a lot of tragedy in her family over the years. Her husband committed suicide and both sons were killed in accidents.

I had accepted the fact that Chet could not get a divorce. You might say he lived a double life. He lived with his parents, spending time with his four children up north as well as visiting us in Columbus. A lot of his income went to support the other kids. I never relied on anything from Chet. He helped when he was able. I loved him in spite of all the turmoil.

He had rented a large rooming house in Charleston, West Virginia and wanted me to move down there. I would be a full time mother. After I agreed, he moved us to 306 Ruffner Avenue, where I changed the bedding and cleaned the rooms rented to the students going to school nearby. The college students were interesting. One in particular was a couple from Egypt. They occasionally used my kitchen to cook meals for their holidays.

Gayle went to school and I stayed home with Joyce. She always wanted to help me.

Chet bought a boxer dog. Joyce loved to play
with him. We had a sandbox in the back
yard and a large front porch with a swing. I
met the mothers of some of Gayle's friends.
Some mornings we'd get together for coffee to
discuss our lives. For about a year everything
went well. We were provided for. Chet would
make the trips up north and back. I enjoyed
living there.

The steel strike began and steel was not
available for the manufacture of tanks—the
next crisis! This meant a big drop in income.
I would have to find a job. To complicate
matters, I was pregnant for the third time.

I wanted to go back to Columbus to work.
The girls and I moved to an upstairs apartment
on North High Street across from the Big Bear
grocery store. It was a handy location with
large rooms. I was rehired by the Bureau of
Unemployment and also started selling Avon
products. Thelma was my baby sitter again.

When my water broke on a Sunday, my doctor was out of town. Thelma called the emergency. I was carried downstairs on a chair. Don was delivered by an intern. Jesse Golding, my friend at work, stayed overnight with the girls while I was in the hospital. Thelma kept Gayle and Joyce during the day. She also delivered my Avon orders in the neighborhood and collected amounts due.

The next move was to an apartment on Third Avenue. We had two floors and a basement, much needed space. The girls went to Second Avenue School and a neighbor kept Don. It was during this period that Chet disappeared. I had no idea what happened. Some time later I found out that he was in prison in West Virginia on a forgery charge. This had something to do with the tanks he sold. Apparently Chet cashed a check belonging to the manufacturer who got angry and pressed charges against him. It could have been worked out amicably, but

Chet lost his temper. To make matters worse he said nasty things and paid the price.

I was taking the bus daily to work at the Crane Company on West Third Avenue. It was time to take driving lessons and get a license. My brother, Joe, bought me a Ford and I started driving to work. Some cold mornings the car wouldn't start, as it was parked on the street. I had good neighbors who would come out and help start my car so I could get to work.

Most of my neighbors were on welfare, got food stamps and clothing free, and also owned cars. I had the opportunity to get welfare too, but turned it down. I chose to work. I took classes in the evenings and got a real estate license—the first step to home ownership.

I bought a house on Ontario Street in a better neighborhood. It required a small down payment. It was a one-floor ranch needing lots of work. The kids and I cleaned and painted everything. We had a yard and a dog.

Our next house on Karl Road was a big improvement. It was one and a half story with a basement, a large porch, a driveway and a huge back yard. We lived there through the kids' teen years. We went to the Methodist Church on Cleveland Avenue where I taught Sunday school. The kids went to the pool within walking distance or they could ride their bikes. Don was on the swim team. Joyce did water ballet.

My three kids attended three different schools, being born four years apart—elementary, middle and high school, so I had to attend events at three different places. In addition to my full-time job with the Federal Government, I got a job at Northland Lazarus part-time evenings and Saturday.

Gayle graduated from Brookhaven and went job hunting. She got an office job with the government. On her resume she had to list her previous addresses. In 17 years we had

moved 22 times. In the early years we'd move
two or three times a year.

By the time the three kids had left home,
we had lived at our house on Karl Road for ten
happy years. The kids all had chores so that
on weekends we could have fun going places.
Gayle had her driving license which helped.
Every summer we'd take vacations.

On one vacation to Florida we stopped
in Kingston, Tennessee and stayed with the
Murrays. Helen Murray and I had worked
together years ago and remained friends. One
summer the kids and I drove all the way to
Los Angeles, California and stayed with Aunt
Vera. She took us to Disneyland, Knotts Berry
Farm and other places of interest. We drove
through the mountains on roads with hair pin
turns and steep drop-offs at the side of the
road.

We stopped in the drifted desert and the
kids got out and ran through the sand. The

temperature was over 100 degrees. We stopped at a restaurant where it was 90 degrees and felt cool. Gayle drove in Nevada where there was no speed limit. I was driving in New Mexico and was pulled over. I had exceeded the 35 mile limit. It was either pay the fine or go to jail. I paid.

On the way back we stopped at a casino in Reno, Nevada. Since Gayle was under 21, I played her coins for her and won. We also visited the Anderson family in Denver, Colorado where we lived when Joyce was born.

4 Tie the Knot

My phone number was always in the phone book. When we lived on Ontario Street, I had a surprise phone call from Chet. I hadn't heard from him in two years. He filled me in on the details of his absence. I had given up on ever hearing from him again. It was over. Now I had to deal with it again. After all, he was the father of my children. I was a wreck! What to do! He coaxed and pleaded. I agreed to see him and it turned into regular visits, but nothing more.

Now, he was living with a woman in the north end of Columbus. She had helped him finalize his divorce papers expecting Chet to marry her. He had other plans. The kids and I had moved to Karl Road. They did not like him. I rarely answered the phone, so whenever Chet called, they said I wasn't home. I didn't know about the calls.

One day when I was alone the phone rang. It was Chet. He wanted to see me. I refused. He kept calling. He was now living alone. He wanted to talk to me. I still had a soft spot in my heart for him. After a few visits, he asked to move in with me. By now, Gayle was on her own and Joyce was away at college. Only Don was living at home. I gave Chet an ultimatum. Either we get married or forget it.

At this stage of Chet's life he was driving a cab. He also owned a race horse, Twin Shot, who was boarding on a farm in Grove City. We made plans to get married. I took time off and we drove to Clintwood, Virginia. On June 29, 1971 we became husband and wife. Chet moved in. He made some rules that Don wasn't happy with. Don finished 12th grade that summer and moved out. He started playing saxophone with a group. Gayle found a "housekeeping" room (now known as an efficiency apartment) on Patterson Avenue for Don and he enrolled at OSU. I paid his tuition and Gayle looked after him.

I sold the house on Karl Road and bought a small farm on Lithopolis Road in Groveport. Chet retired and became a thoroughbred horse trainer. We bought more horses.

I started walking Twin Shot. He gave me a hard time. Animals can sense fear. Chet insisted I do it. He said eventually I would enjoy walking horses. He was right.

Thoroughbreds are high-strung, however, some of them have better temperaments than others. I learned to take control. We bought a mare and had her bred. We raised two of her foals. I cleaned stalls, put the horses out to pasture, fed and watered them. I loved them all, went to the races, bet on them and read the racing form, as well as meeting other owners and trainers. This was far different than anything I had ever done.

I still had my job with the Department of Defense. Chet took the horses to Florida in the winter. He also raced in Chicago, Kentucky, Canada and of course Beulah Park in Grove City as well as the other two race tracks in Cleveland and Cincinnati, Ohio. There was never a dull moment. It was such a thrill when one of our horses won a race. Our best horse, "Pins Babby", who we bought in Kentucky, paid off the farm.

For the twelve years we were legally married, we had many good times traveling and doing other various activities. I was devastated when he died in the spring of 1983. I had lost the love of my life.

5   Camp Mary Orton

My three kids and I went to camp, the summer of 1960. I was between jobs and Chet wasn't around. I had applied for assistance and received some funds. I was told I could stay at home and go on "welfare."

I told them, "No, I'm sorry, I can't do that. I intend to find a job."

The counselor suggested the camp. They helped with the expenses. This was a real break! I bought yard goods and sewed four pairs of identical shorts for each of us in four different colors. I also bought other necessary items and off we went. Here we met other mothers and children of all ages. What a wonderful gift! Everyone had a good time.

The counselors and mothers wrote articles for "The Log of Camp Mary Orton." It was typed up and we all received copies. I wrote the following:

"Our Swinging Mothers"

Last night we camped out at Johnson Lodge. We built a fire in the huge fireplace and hauled in logs. The children roasted marshmallows and were bedded down. Mothers played "pig" till the wee hours, and then turned in. It was a hard floor but we made it. For breakfast we had cereal, hot chocolate, bacon and eggs, coffee and toast made in a popcorn popper over the fireplace. Everyone had a good time.

Our cabins are looking much better with the curtains going up all over Mothers Camp, thanks to Mrs. Moore.

The boys from an older group of Boy Scouts and Camp Lazarus put on an Indian Show at the Recreation Hall the night it rained. Mothers and children thoroughly enjoyed it. We thought we might put on a water ballet but someone is always sinking so we've given it up.

Everyone is enjoying cafeteria style eating. Those who have been here before say it's a big improvement. Other changes this year do not seem as favorable such as not having the boys around. They are much missed by all. General opinion seems to be that everyone would like to see them back. You see, mothers do a lot of talking and if you need any opinions just ask us.

6 My Three Jewels

They are Gayle, Joyce and Don. They arrived four years apart—two daughters in September of 1948 and 1952 and my son in November of 1956. Each of them have been a joy with different temperaments and personalities. For four years Gayle had my undivided attention. When Joyce arrived attention was divided in two and with Don, a three-way split.

Gayle was so happy to have a sister. She played with Joyce and pushed her in the stroller. If Joyce cried, Gayle would talk to her and settle her down. I sewed a lot and made them sister dresses. Gayle became a responsible person at an early age, as I always had a job. I could not depend on an income from Chet. The only time I was a stay-at-home mom was when we lived in Charleston, West Virginia for about two years.

Joyce resented my having to work. It was an era when most mothers stayed at home. Being raised by a single parent was not as common as it is today. I always had responsible baby-sitters. When I no longer needed them, Gayle was in charge. I'd have to leave before they left for school, I couldn't see them off. It was not a matter of choice.

I imagine that was a deciding factor in Joyce's marriage. Joyce and Steve met at a fast food restaurant where they both worked. Some months later, Steve proposed and they had an outdoor wedding at the farm. They had one daughter, Stephanie, and Joyce chose to stay at home. My son-in-law, Steve, had to bring home the bacon. During the summer, Joyce would work at the pool, giving swim lessons and Stephanie would be there with her.

All three of my kids had memberships at Linden Beach and went to the pool often while they were growing up. Joyce became a good swimmer at an early age. Don made the swim team and I'd go to swim meets. I got Don a membership at the YWCA where he'd go swimming the rest of the year.

Joyce got her temperament from Chet and her attitude from me. No one tells me what to do and it's that way with Joyce. She also has my optimism. I bought a used piano and started both girls on piano lessons. They were not interested.

Don would climb up on the piano bench and gently touch the keys when he was two years old. He became the musician. When he was in the fourth grade he wanted a saxophone. I told him I would rent one and if he learned to play well enough I'd buy one. I also told him I'd never ask him to practice. If he really wanted to play the sax he'd have to do it on his own. Well, he did! In the sixth grade he composed music and went on to became a good musician.

Don graduated from high school at the age of 16 and has been on his own ever since.

He studied music at OSU, but dropped out and went on the road playing gigs. One day, he reflected on his life and he decided he needed structure. Don auditioned and passed the necessary tests and became a member of the US Army Band. He went through basic training at Ft. Knox, Kentucky. He chose to go to Germany to play sax in the US Army Band and met Janice DeWolfe. They got married in Stuttgart where their first child, Jason, was born.

After Don completed his service, he enrolled at Indiana University in Bloomington, Indiana where he got his degree. Janice played the French horn and got her degree at Julliard in New York. They are both good musicians and have equally good minds. While they lived in family housing at IU, Janice got her Master's Degree. Their daughter, Marilyn, was born in Indianapolis, Indiana, while Don was completing his service at Ft. Benjamin Harrison.

I had retired from the Federal Government by this time and was living in Bexley. Don asked me if I would consider baby-sitting for them while they finished their degrees. I agreed to do it and every Monday I'd drive to Bloomington. On weekends I would drive home. Gayle wondered if I could handle Don's two small children since I always had baby-sitters for my children. No problem. It worked out beautifully. I enjoyed the kids.

On campus, I slept downstairs in the living room and lived out of a suitcase. Once a week, I cooked the evening meal. I gave the kids their lunches and played with them. Don and Janice took care of the laundry, housework, dishes etc. and studied. Some weekends I would bring the children home with me. They were well behaved and sat in their car seats in the back while I drove.

Janice saw to it that I could attend musical programs on campus. I really enjoyed attending their performances. When they graduated I applied to the Peace Corps. Of all the applicants, only 26% got accepted. After all the paperwork and interviews they gave me an assignment. That's another chapter or two.

After Don and Janice got their degrees they moved in with me while they went job hunting. Jason started school in Bexley. Next, they rented a half double in the north end. Eventually they bought a house in Utica where the kids went to a nearby school. Don now had a career position with the Department of Defense. Janice stayed involved with music. She played the organ at church, taught piano lessons, played the horn with local music groups and played piano for the ballet-met where both kids took ballet lessons.

Gayle also attended OSU for a short period but chose not to stick with it. She and Joyce lived in an apartment in the campus area. Joyce had enrolled at Kent State University but dropped out before she had completed her first year. Both sisters did some job hopping going from one thing to another. This eventually led to their marriages.

Gayle was a waitress when she met Bob. She became his secretary when he passed the bar and was getting his start as a lawyer. They too got married. Bob had a son, Fred, from his previous marriage. Gayle became Freddie's mom. Fred passed the bar a few years ago and is also practicing law. He is married to Molly and they have a little boy named Nickie.

Joyce's daughter, Stephanie, is married to Andrew. They have three daughters, Anabelle, Bailey and Chloey. Joyce has her own business as a real estate appraiser. She is an independent business woman. She has come a long way, putting her good mind to use. The real estate market is slow since the economy has dipped, but Joyce manages to keep busy on other projects.

I had returned from the Peace Corps in
1993 and Don's two children were again
spending time with grandma. I'd pick them
up after ballet lessons on Saturday and they
would stay overnight. We had such a good
time together, playing cards or scrabble. We'd
go shopping or to the movies. Late Sunday I'd
drive them back to Utica.

In the meantime Janice, Don's wife, joined
the Army Reserves and played the French
horn. Every summer she'd be gone for annual
training. The kids spent most of this time with
me. We went travelling to Cancun, the Cayman
Islands and Hawaii during the summers. My
retirement income was enough to do whatever
they wanted to do. Needless to say, the credit
cards got a lot of use.

It was time to move on. Don applied for
a position in Battle Creek, Michigan with the
Department of Defense moving up the ladder.
They bought a house there and relocated.

Now I would see them even less. I still drive
five hours from time to time to spend a few
days visiting. I've attended their graduations
from high school and college and attended
athletic events they were participating in such
as baseball, basketball and track.

Don's next assignment was in Germany as
a customer service representative supplying
the armed services with necessities—another
promotion. This involved sophisticated
computer use, which is Don's field of expertise.
Later assignments required spending time in
Iraq and other countries in Asia where the US
Military is involved. My grandson, Jason, and
I visited him in Bahrain, off the coast in Saudi
Arabia. It was Mother's Day in 2009.

7 The Grandchildren

One of the greatest pleasures of being a grandma is taking the kids traveling. I took Stephanie on a cruise. We flew to Florida and got on the ship of Premier Cruise Lines. It was the first time she had ever been on a plane. We had a great time!

I never took my oldest grandchild, Fred, on a trip, but we went to a lot of movies together. The other two, Jason and Marilyn, went on several trips with me. They were well-behaved, courteous and loved to talk to strangers. They wanted to try everything. Eating was no problem. We'd go to restaurants, fast food or pick up snacks. We went to Hawaii, the Cayman Islands and Mexico during the summer months.

The trips ended when they had to earn money. As they grew older, the spring breaks meant going south with their friends. They went to college, got degrees and got married.

Jason is engaged and they are planning their wedding. He is an assistant volley ball coach for the women's volley ball team at Western University of Michigan.

Marilyn got married in July 2010 and is employed doing research in Kalamazoo, Michigan.

Fred and his wife have a baby boy. He is a lawyer.

Stephanie and her husband have three daughters and own a pizza business.

AUG • 71

8 Dogs and Cats

Chet liked boxers. When we lived on Karl Road we went to Marysville to see some boxer pups. One of them was white with some black around one eye. Because of this he could not be registered with the kennel club and we got him at a bargain price. He'd already had his ears clipped.

Chet trained him. What a wonder dog Duke was. Fourteen years later, Chet told me he had lived longer than most boxers and possibly would not live much longer. As it turned out, Chet died first. Duke was a good watch dog. His growl scared people. No one entered the house unless I wanted them to.

My kids did not like me living alone on the farm. I would not consider moving until Duke died around the end of the year. I cried as I had lost a friend. Now, I would consider moving.

Another dog we had at the farm was Sam, a smaller outdoor dog. One of Chet's friends wanted to give him to us. Chet said no. One day I came home from work and he was tied out back. There was a note which read: "His name is Sam." We had him for ten years. One day he was hit by a car. I buried him behind the barn.

Another casualty was a poodle. Gayle and Bob had to let him go because of Bob's allergies. He also was killed by a car. We had numerous cats, in addition to horses.

A friend gave us a beautiful indoor cat who loved to sit on Chet's lap. He'd go out and come right back in. The others were barn cats. We fed them all. While I was growing up, we always had a cat or two. Dad liked them. They took care of the mice. Through the years there were other dogs and cats. I love animals.

After Duke died, I moved to Bexley, Ohio and traveled. No pets and no plants, except the lone cactus that lives on to this day from sheer neglect. The kids felt I should have a dog, as I lived alone and had been robbed twice. What for? There was no jewelry left. Luckily, the insurance covered my loss. I replaced a few items that were stolen. After the second time, they cancelled my policy. For five years I had no insurance and couldn't get any.

One day as I was chatting with my neighbor, Betty, across the street, along came this young lady walking her dog.

We both commented, "What a beautiful dog!"

She said, "Do you want him? He's available."

They got him in Mexico. He'd been a beach bum, who befriended them. One thing led to another and after necessary shots, he flew back with Barb and her husband. However their two dogs at home did not like Kai. He had to go. She even had him spayed. All she wanted for him was a good home, no charge. Kai had a good home with me, as I moved from one place to another. He adjusted well and was a good watch dog. Every morning we walked no matter what the weather. When I travelled, he went to Doran's Kennel, his second home.

Kai died in 2007. A few months later I got Hillary, a young beagle, from the animal shelter.

9   The Moves

I worked at DCSC until January 9, 1984,
the day I was eligible to retire. After Chet died
in April 1983, I sold the horses. My white
boxer, Duke, died in November of 1983. I
buried him under the big maple tree out back.
The kids had been after me to move to the city.
They did not want me living out there alone.
Now that Duke was gone, I would consider it.

After the holidays I put the farm up for sale.
Interest rates were at an all time high of 12%.
Real estate was at a standstill. The secretary
at Gayle and Bob's law office on Neil Avenue
told her about an available house in Bexley
with low rent. The secretary's mother-in-law
who had lived in that house died. Gayle got in
touch with the owner and rented the house for
me on Grandon Avenue for $150 a month.

During the next five months I lived in two places. I'd load the car and haul boxes. I had a huge garage sale. Moving to a smaller house required downsizing. Eventually, I sold the farm on land contract. After 12 years it had doubled in price. Everything got paid off and I had money left to travel.

For 16 years, the twin sisters who owned the property never raised the rent. When they went into assisted living they sold all their properties to a conglomerate that tripled the rent. They would let me stay for three months at $450, and then rent would go up to $600. The house had a few problems, but I never complained about anything. Whenever something needed fixing I paid to have it done. If we had a heavy rainy season, the basement flooded, so I never kept anything on the floor. The new owner had been told by the sisters that I was the best tenant they ever had.

The next residence was in Whitehall on Beechwood Avenue. It was a half double with basement and a fenced yard at $525 monthly. My neighbors were Henry and Val Housemann. I liked them, but I felt cramped. There was no garage, a double driveway and cars parked everywhere. No one owned just one car!

After a year the rent went to $540. I still traveled. I took courses at Columbus State College. At a seminar I attended, I learned that I could buy a house—with no down payment—called the "Ameridream" program.

In the spring, I started looking for houses. When I told my children they had a fit. Why would I take on the responsibility of a house? I didn't need these negative vibes. I quit talking about it. I found the house I wanted with a lovely finished basement at a price I could afford. I was preapproved for a $75,000 loan. The neighborhood wasn't the best, but the houses were decent.

I signed the contract and started packing boxes. After the closing I called moving companies for estimates. My monthly payment on a 30-year loan was $595 at 6.4%. At age 80, I was once again a homeowner. I called the kids and gave them my new address on Weyant Avenue but kept the same phone number.

After two years I moved into another house in Bexley, Ohio on Cassingham Road. It took three moves, but I was back where I wanted to be in a lovely neighborhood. This house was only two miles west of my previous home with a price difference of $50,000. My mortgage payments are almost double from the last mortgage, but I have adequate income to manage all my needs. Of course, I'll cut down on my travel expenses by taking cheaper trips. Having traveled on all the continents, fulfilling one of my goals, I no longer will travel so extensively.

As I reflect on how all this came to pass, I know it's because I set goals and never doubted that I would reach them. When I found the house I wanted, I got a realtor for the house on Weyant. I made a special trip to St. Theresa's Convent on East Broad Street and bought a small St. Joseph statue and buried it in the front yard. I had read about this being helpful in house sales.

Within three days I had a buyer. I never allowed any negative thoughts to enter the picture. On June 30th I had the closing on the house I sold and bought my new home on the same day. The following day I moved. Throughout all of this, I worked every day at my part-time job for two months. I had faith and a positive mental attitude that it would all work out and it did.

I love this neighborhood. People are friendly and courteous. I sit on the front porch on my wicker furniture and read or watch the cars go by. My dog is out there, too. Sometimes I sit on the deck next to my spare room and read.

I have a fenced backyard so the dog can roam without a chain. A young man, Jed, lives in the carpeted basement. The bathroom is huge with a tub, shower, toilet and a vanity with drawers and mirror. He lived with me at the previous address in the basement, which was also fully furnished. I only go down to the basement now, to do the laundry. Jed is a big help in many ways. He opens jars, lifts or carries heavy items, looks after things when I'm gone and is my computer expert. Whenever I have a computer problem, he knows exactly how to solve it.

My current home also has an attic with flooring where all the boxes and other stuff I don't need are stored. The rest of the accumulation is in the garage. The cement driveway is big enough for two cars. My kitchen has a built-in gas stove and adequate counter space and cupboards. The rooms are smaller than my previous home, but cozy with hard wood floors.

10   Travels

Retirement is a time for unfulfilled dreams. As a youngster, I always longed to travel. Geography was my favorite subject. My family had no car. The only trip we took was to a funeral in Pittsburgh, Pennsylvania by train. During my working years we traveled in the states. Worldwide travel would come later. When my eligibility day arrived in January 1984, I signed my retirement papers and began to fulfill my lifelong dreams.

My first trip was to Hawaii with my former baby-sitter, Thelma. Traveling to all the continents was my goal. After several trips to various places, I applied as a volunteer to the Peace Corps in 1987. I had done volunteer work at different places, including the Salvation Army, and felt qualified. This was a long process involving interviews and

paper work. Finally, about a year later, I
received the invitation to attend orientation.
My assignment would be Agriculture.

In the fall of 1989, I was in the Philippines
on the island of Catanduanes for about six
months. My hut did not have running water,
electricity or bath. In 1990, we were evacuated.
The US Embassy arranged flights to Hawaii,
where 261 volunteers were out-processed.

After spending a week at the University of
Hawaii and sightseeing around the islands, I
was not ready to go home. I had decided to
visit Australia after my tour of duty. Plans
changed, so now was the time to go. I bought a
ticket and was on my way to Australia. I stayed
at the YMCA and at youth hostels where I met
friendly travelers of all ages who advised the
best places to visit at the most economical
prices. Next trip was to New Zealand where
the adventures continued.

During my travels, the Peace Corps mailed
to my home an invitation for an assignment

in Africa, but I was not available. Evacuated volunteers had priority placement to go elsewhere. When I returned home, I requested Costa Rica. I received an assignment in Community Development.

Prior to our departure, during a three-day orientation in Miami, instructors informed us of the many phases of life in Costa Rica. I had the opportunity to experience the lifestyles of both Costa Ricans and the Indians by the time I had completed my assignment.

It was necessary to become proficient in Spanish to receive an assignment. The test was oral and consisted of a 20-minute conversation with the examiner in Spanish. It was one of the most agonizing things I have ever done.

When we were sworn in, the first order of business was to open a checking account. No one spoke English. In my second year, my checks were stolen. That was a major problem.

First of all, I had to fill out forms. The bank requires that you run an ad in the newspaper about the stolen checks at your own expense, before they will issue new checks. The Peace Corps requires that you report to the police department and fill out more forms, of course, in Spanish.

For three months, while in training in Alajuela, we practiced speaking daily in class, and at home with the family we lived with who spoke no English. Daily living was done entirely in Spanish.

On the reservation, word usage was somewhat different. I had a tutor teach me the expressions and words I didn't understand. Professional people are the easiest to converse with. They've dealt with non-Spanish speakers and talk slower and more distinctly. Most Costa Ricans run their words together. As time went on, it became easier for me. Later, when I traveled to Spain, I was able to communicate quite well. There are just a few differences in pronunciation.

Upon successful completion of a three month training program in Costa Rica, which included conversational Spanish, trans-cultural orientation and technical training, I received my assignment. My village was in Quitirrisi, an Indian Reservation, which was an hour and a half by bus from the capital, San Jose, up winding roads into the mountains.

My project was Integrated Community Development. This required adapting my skills to the community needs. I was to analyze and involve myself in their methods, and communicate with the officials. The 12-week training concentrated on organizational skills and how to effectively transfer information using non-formal or formal techniques. It was necessary to become adequately proficient in Spanish to be able to live and function as a volunteer. In Quitirrisi, no one spoke English.

I rented the only house available and negotiated the terms. The cement blockhouse had a tin roof and needed improvements. Using candles and carrying water, I settled in. I shopped for minimal necessities. After three weeks, I had electricity, water, a toilet and a shower.

I became immersed in the community by attending meetings, social functions and visiting families. Of priority importance was the establishment of a kindergarten. That required taking a census and collecting the names and birthdates of children, ages five and six. A young mother, who directed me to the various homes spaced far apart on the mountain, accompanied me. After I had interviewed thirty families, a health worker from the next town informed me that the birth records were available in his office.

The next step was to go to the Ministry of Education with my counterpart, who was also the mayor. We presented the list to the officials in San Jose. At first, they were not willing to provide a kindergarten teacher. After two more visits, they relented and we were ready to start. We selected a building that was being used for other purposes and made arrangements to paint and clean. I solicited funding from a group in the US for tables and chairs. I negotiated with a local manufacturer to build them and arrange for delivery. When I completed my service as a Peace Corps volunteer, the kindergarten was operating successfully.

The Indians wanted to learn English to be able to improve their lives. I developed lessons and instructed students and adults in special classes. I obtained seeds from the Kellogg Foundation, contributed to their funds for the needy and shared cultural information with them. It was a pleasure to participate in their celebrations, attend weddings, christenings and funerals, and became immersed in the life on the reservation.

I acquired an education in the various
cultural aspects of life in Costa Rica and
had the opportunity to visit various historic
and ecological areas. By attending concerts
and various Costa Rican events in San Jose,
I became familiar with their literature and
music of the various Indians and Costa Ricans.
I traveled to volcanoes, forests, coffee and
banana plantations, the Atlantic and Pacific
seashores, National Parks and churches. I
learned to do a job in a culture far removed
from my own and successfully completed my
assignment.

The differences in culture are unique. Daily
chores consist of cleaning floors first thing
in the morning. Children are precious and
pampered. They are carried everywhere even
after they can walk. One sees few strollers
anywhere.

There is adequate, though crowded, bus
service almost everywhere. Most people ride

buses. Men will give up a seat on a crowded bus to a woman carrying a child or to an older woman. To walk a mile or two is not uncommon. Taxis are available but it is necessary to negotiate the fare before getting in. Some workers in the service industry have the image of the rich American and try to get all they can.

Open-air markets are many. Fresh fruits and vegetables are always available. At the restaurants, one can eat much cheaper if ordering Costa Rican dishes. In the larger cities, you'll find fast foods such as Pizza Hut, McDonalds or Kentucky Fried Chicken, but they cost more than the local meals.

Private doctors are available to those who can pay. Most doctors have studied in the US. Their office hours start after 2:00 p.m., as they are required to go to the clinics in the morning. The clinics are crowded. There are no appointments. I had a blood clot dissolved in a doctor's office and walked out with a bandage on my leg. I had a similar incident 20 years ago and had to stay off my feet. I missed two weeks of work.

Costa Ricans love music. The National Symphony plays one weekend a month at the National Theater. On Sunday mornings, the admission is reduced making it possible for anyone to attend. Generally, there's a long waiting line. One gets used to waiting in banks, post offices, supermarkets or bus lines. Concerts in parks are free. The Marimba band on the reservation played for all the celebrations. In San Jose, musicians play in various places. The audience stands around and listens and drops money in a box. At the Cultural Plaza, musicians entertain every weekend to large crowds.

I learned to be alert in crowds as thievery is rampant. More than once, I was bumped, but I never lost anything, however, there were numerous close calls. Two of my friends had expensive sunglasses stolen off their faces. Others had necklaces ripped off their necks. It isn't customary for thieves to carry guns, so there are few violent crimes. Material things are replaceable.

During my stay in Quitirrisi, I had participated in a course given by two Iowa State professors entitled *Community Development, Leadership and Communication*. We went to Guapilis, Costa Rica one Monday afternoon and left on Friday. We stayed in dorms with three bathrooms for 15 people. We ate Costa Rican meals as a group, family style and spoke Spanish.

Classes started on Monday evening and we immediately plunged into the issues. Each participant drew pictures and flip charts to illustrate conditions in their individual communities. We also did role-plays to point out how to effectively deal with problems in the community.

One of my presentations was concerning a much needed parking area on the highway where the Indians sold their products and handiwork. I took the drawings and flip charts back with me and discussed it with the leaders. I drew up a plan showing the suggested location and how to accomplish the task.

They listened and agreed with the idea, but because this was the rainy season not many projects were accomplished. The equipment available was used for mudslides as needed. Workers were paid 100 colones an hour and extra funds were not available. This was a poor community and progress was very slow. When I visited a few years later, no one had undertaken the project, even though they were aware of how the parking lot would benefit them.

One successful Fair event was arranged by a group of volunteers. We set up booths in the community hall of a church using maps and displays depicting life in the United States. Flyers were prepared and distributed. The community had a chance to meet the "gringos." Despite the rain, the hall was packed. Families from babies to grandparents came. It was a wonderful way to mix with the locals.

I met Peg in the Peace Corps when we were in the Philippines in 1989 and we have taken many trips together. One of my extensive trips was on the Trans-Siberian Railway with Peg. I kept a diary and when we returned she typed it up. We were gone for a month in the summer of 1996. She lived in Hartford, Connecticut. We met at JFK in New York and flew to Helsinki, Finland. After a few days, we flew to Beijing, China and toured there.

Of special interest was The Great Wall of China, which we climbed. My local travel agent arranged our stops so that we would visit the places of interest before moving on.

We boarded the train in China and got off in Mongolia, Siberia and Moscow. A different travel agent would be at each stop and take us to our hotel and arrange sightseeing tours.

The train went from Beijing through the Gobi Desert to Mongolia. We got off to visit the National Museum and other sites. Then on to Siberia to see Lake Baikal. It was the last leg of our journey through Siberia when we met Leonard. He was traveling alone. Peg and I had a compartment four doors down. Our door was always open in case anyone wanted to stop on their way to the samovar. Peg and I commented to each other that the man walking past our door looked like Boris Yeltson, so we asked him.

"No, I'm Leonard," he said.

I wanted his picture so Peg got the camera. We talked back and forth. He spoke in Russian, Peg and I, in English. Neither of us could understand the other's language, but we smiled a lot.

At the next train stop Leonard got off and bought something for us. It was wrapped in newspaper. We thanked him. When we opened the gift, we discovered it was smoked herring. What were we going to do with smoked herring? For the first time, we closed the door. Peg found her Swiss army knife and started cutting. It was raw and smelled. I knew I wasn't going to eat it, neither was Peg. After cutting it up into small pieces, we wrapped it in several plastic bags and back into the newspaper.

As we tossed it into the trash, we agreed, "It's the thought that counts."

We crossed Asia into Europe and got off in Moscow, toured the area and got a flight to Paris. We took a cab to the hotel where we got a senior citizen rate.

The next morning, we went out to breakfast and took the Metro to the Champs Elysees. From there we walked to the Eiffel Tower and to the Arc de Triompe. Then we went back to the railroad station to board the Metro back to the hotel. We stopped at Burger King for hamburgers and french fries. Then to the grocery store to buy wine, bread and bananas, as we still had peanut butter and jelly left in the room.

The next day, we visited Notre Dame Cathedral and the Grand Palace. We took the train to Euro-Disney and walked through Fantasy World. Back at the hotel we watched CNN and played Skipbo. The following morning we checked out, got a cab to the airport and flew back to the US.

11   Education

After having to drop out of Youngstown College in 1940, I wanted to continue my education. Years later I attended Ohio State University and Columbus Community College. After discussion with my counselor, I selected Psychology for my degree work. I've had years of volunteer work at college level caliber in the area of business and human resources. My major was multi-disciplinary with focus on business and psychology. I wanted to become involved in counseling immigrants. I can communicate in Spanish and I have tutored Chinese immigrants.

Another area of my experience is money management and budgeting. I've been reading articles about how this generation has financial problems, due to living without a budget. Having grown up during the depression, I manage money well. I've had lean years in the past and now in retirement survive on less income, traveling and living economically. Being realistic, getting a degree is just not that important any more.

In the summer of 1994, I wrote several articles to receive credit for lifetime experience, while I attended Capital University. After completing a few courses, I decided not to continue. I had paid $1500 for two classes. Way too expensive! My choice was to travel and I could not afford both.

Later, I took classes at Columbus State, formerly Columbus Community College. For seniors, tuition and parking was free. There were minimal lab fees and books that could be sold when no longer needed. I've accumulated a lot of credit hours. Later I would only audit the classes, as tests were too stressful. I was on the Dean's list by this time and did not want to drive myself anymore. Maybe it was time to get over my competitive nature.

12   Camping

In the fall of 1996, Peg and I decided to go camping in the national parks and invited another friend, Emily, to come with us. My dog went to the kennel and we spent a month on the road. I took notes along the way and Peg did the typing again when we returned. Peg had leadership qualities and it was her car. She mailed instructions. This is a follow-up on the previous 56 memos we received from her.

It read: "Be packed and ready to leave at 8:00 a.m. Tuesday. Due to lack of space, pack lightly. Eliminate unnecessary items. Camping does not require dress clothes. Weather being unpredictable, pack both warm and light clothing, two outfits each. Remember layering helps take off the chill.

As for food, only minimal amounts are needed, as we'll be stopping at supermarkets to buy fruits, vegetables and other food items. We'll stop at laundromats as needed.

Roll your sleeping bag and air mattress tightly to conserve space. Some reading material and cards help pass time after dark. The lantern will provide light. A few extra items such as t-shirts, shoes and underwear are practical. Anything forgotten can be purchased along the way."

My daughter, Gayle, had doubts about how the three of us would get along. We made the trip with no personal upsets and are still friends today. One mishap did provide much conversation along the way, after a buffalo smashed into the car. The damage was not enough to stop our trip and after a visit to a garage for a few necessary repairs, we were on our way. Cracked windows and dents could wait until we got home.

It was dusk. The sun was setting. The deer and the buffalo were roaming. Yellowstone

Park was their domain. We were the outsiders. We expected to be out of the park before nightfall; however, we waited for Old Faithful to blow since it had gone off just before we arrived. Word was that it would gush again in 45 minutes. Despite the chill, we chose to wait. As it turned out, it was an hour and a half later.

Rushing to our car, we headed out. Too late! It was dark now and buffalo were everywhere. One was crossing the road in front of us. We didn't see him. There were no lights in Yellowstone Park. Peg hit the brakes. In a flash, he was on the hood of our car and smashed the windshield. We looked around. The buffalo kept right on crossing the road, apparently unhurt. His only loss was a few hairs embedded in the windshield.

Checking the damage, only one headlight was broken. About ten inches of the windshield was unbroken on the driver's side. We were lucky, we realized as we drove on out. Several people rushed over to see if anyone was hurt. They hugged us in relief. A young man on the opposite side of the road had been flashing his lights to warn us when he saw the buffalo, but we thought perhaps someone was in trouble and signaling for help.

We came to a KOA and were able to rent a cabin in the middle of nowhere. It was cold, about 40 degrees. They gave us a heater and there were blankets in the car. The bathroom was across from our cabin and clean. The cost was $48. We slept in our clothes. The following day we drove through snow, sleet and hail on the way to Grand Teton.

We left Wyoming and entered Idaho, scraped ice off the windshield and spent the next night in a motel. Just over the border in Utah, we had to stop for a herd of sheep led by an Indian on horseback. Peg had called her friend, Val, in Morgan, Utah so we stayed with

her the following night. Val drove us around to
see the fabulous mountain views. On Sunday,
we went to the Mormon Tabernacle and heard
the choir that happened to be broadcasting
while we were in attendance. Upon leaving
we saw six tour buses, loads of people and a
parking lot full of cars, all there to hear the
broadcast.

We went on to Bryce Canyon, where we
pitched our tent. The red rock formations
were magnificent. The elevation is 7400
feet. We had soup and sandwiches for supper
and played Skipbo. All the campgrounds at
our next stop, the Grand Canyon, were full.
The cabin we rented cost $82.08, our most
expensive stay. We had two rooms with three
beds and a bath. We disconnected the smoke
alarm so we could cook. The scenery was
breathtaking! Deer darted across the road.
RV's everywhere. Our corrugated car elicited
a lot of interest. We kept repeating the story

of the buffalo and people would shake their heads in amazement.

Camp at Flagstaff, Arizona cost $4.00. No frost here. We played cards and roasted marshmallows. Navajos sold their arts and crafts. We drove west on the scenic route to California two days later. Huge Joshua trees came into view and later we saw magnificent Sequoias where we camped. The tall beautiful trees were quite a sight. Here campsites were $6.00. Many tourists from Germany and England camped in this area. We left no food in the car and kept the windows open to prevent the bears from breaking in, as they were always around looking for food.

Priscilla, our friend, who was also in the Peace Corps with us, lived in Stockton, California—our next stop. We toured sights such as the famed Napa Valley and the Golden Gate Bridge in San Francisco. On our way to the Grand Canyon we stopped at Indian

Reservations. When we headed back east, we took the southern route stopping and camping in New Mexico and Texas and other places of interest.

The tent and folding chairs went on top of the car. There was limited space left after sleeping bags and air mattresses. Peg insisted that we do no shopping along the way, except bare necessities. Emily and I did manage to pick up a few souvenirs. When we returned Gayle said she couldn't believe the three of us were still speaking to each other, but we were. It was a fabulous trip. I kept track of the expenses, using my credit card. After dividing it three ways, it had cost each of us $500.

13   Employment

As I write the story of my life, there are gaps. I've mentioned some of my jobs. In this chapter, I'll try to fill in the missing. For a while in 1947, when I lived with Aunt Vera in Los Angeles, I had worked for the phone company as an operator. From 1948 to 1950, I was a file clerk with the Bureau of Unemployment Compensation in Columbus. Next I was an account clerk at the Board of Education. Later, I took a test and got my first Federal Government job entitled Accounting Technician from 1962 to 1968. I took the Federal Service Entrance Exam and was promoted into the career program starting as a GS-5 Contracting Officer. After passing several courses I continued up the ladder to GS-11. The very day I was eligible to retire in January 1984, I signed the papers and was gone.

In addition to my career, I had various
part-time jobs. I sold Avon products, worked
evenings at Lazarus in the garden shop, got a
real estate license and also did some volunteer
work, such as tutoring kids in the inner city.
I am a multi-tasker. I need diversion in my
life. As I review my resume, I notice there are
still some gaps. It's not that easy to put it all
together. How important is it anyway?

In 1951, I moved to Fairborn, Ohio and
worked for the Air Force at Patterson Field.
My daughter, Gayle, and I lived in a trailer park.
Two years later I moved back to Columbus
and worked at Fort Hayes. I transferred to
the Defense Construction Center when Fort
Hayes closed and continued my career there
until I retired.

The only time I was unemployed was when
DCSC had a reduction in force. I was a GS-
9. They offered me a GS-7. I turned it down.
I got severance pay for ten months and then

signed up for unemployment compensation. The layoff was during the winter when Chet was preparing to take the horses to Florida. We closed up the house and I got to spend the entire winter in a warm climate. My checks went to the bank. While in Florida, I was sent a second offer of a GS-7.

"No, thank you. I will only come back for a GS-9," I told them.

Chet thought I was a fool to turn it down.

"They will never offer it to you," he said.

He was wrong. At that time, it was in the dead of winter. Columbus was having its worst winter since 1950. Schools were closed. The governor declared it a disaster.

"I am not going back," I declared.

When the checks stopped, I had to report to the BUC and actively job hunt. By August, Chet was starting to panic. The horses were not winning races, and then the letter came. They called me in for an interview.

Chet said, "That doesn't mean you have the job."

I said, "I'll get it."

I had to pass a physical again. I didn't pass the eye test at first. After I got new glasses, I was hired.

We had a Ford LTD with 93,000 miles on it and would need a new car. I asked Chet if I could pick the car.

"You can have whatever you want," he replied to my request.

The day the letter arrived, I went to the Cadillac Motor Co. and selected my car. Chet could not believe what I did.

"You promised," I said.

"You could have picked a cheaper car," he replied.

"Sorry, this is the car I want!" I said.

I traded in the Ford, got approved by the credit union for a loan and now I had a Cadillac. When I went to get it, I lost my nerve. I had never driven a car so big with all those buttons. I called Chet and asked him to come over with the pickup truck. He drove my new car home. I drove the truck.

I drove up and down the country roads and got comfortable driving my Cadillac. When I started back to work, I had no problem driving my beautiful new car.

There have been times in my life when I have been unemployed, had kids to feed and clothe, but I refused to let it get me down. Problems to me were always challenges, not something to moan about. I always have tried to keep a positive outlook and expected things to work out. To this day, I continue to follow this philosophy and it works.

14 Hungary

In 2002, I visited my distant cousins in Budapest. Kati had come to the US in the 80s. She visited my brother, Joe, and his wife in Youngstown, Ohio. The three of them drove to Groveport where Chet had the farm and horses. After 20 years my friend Hilda, who was born in Hungary, helped me get in touch with Kati. I hadn't spoken the language in years and needed help writing letters.

I was invited to their home. Kati met me at the airport with her son, Palie, who knows some English. I had my Hungarian dictionary with me as my language skills left much to be desired. Palie is a singer in show business and has traveled in the US. We communicated quite well.

The next morning, after breakfast, I announced that I wanted to take a walk. They said okay and gave me the remote for the gate.

Off I went. After walking about a half hour, I turned back. I could not remember which street I had turned off on. They all looked alike. I had no ID—nothing. I remembered their name, but that was all. The family had moved there during the past summer.

Of the different people I stopped, no one knew them. Finally, I met an older couple carrying groceries. I explained my dilemma in broken Hungarian and they understood. She set down her bag and whipped out her cell phone and called the police department. Three men in uniform arrived in a police car. I'm sure they were curious about the lost American, probably thinking a case of Alzheimer's. One of them called Kati's phone number. I recognized her voice immediately. She gave them directions and I was driven home. Kati had begun to worry and was about to go looking for me on her bike.

The cops asked to see my passport.

I asked if I could take their picture and they said, "Of course."

I am now on record in Budapest as "Lost and Found."

Kati's family asked if I was afraid being lost.

I laughed, "No, this is something that happens to me often."

I have no sense of direction. I've traveled the world and always get where I want to be but sometimes, a detour is involved. When I walk out of a hotel room, I always make a wrong turn. A lifetime habit.

15 The Immigrants in Bexley

Soumiya was my new neighbor in 1999. She moved in at the beginning of the school year in September, from Paris, France. Her nationality is Moroccan. She has lived abroad many years due to her husband's work. Mr. B works for the Moroccan Embassy and periodically gets reassigned. He speaks no English. When he visited, our conversation consisted of *bonjour* and *merci*. The three daughters were attending school in Bexley and he was thanking me for helping the family with English. The girls served as interpreters as we spoke.

Mr. B was waiting for his next assignment and went back to the Embassy in Rabat, the capitol. These things go through channels and drag on and on. If nothing were finalized by the end of the school, the family would return to Rabat. Soumiya felt it was time for the children to learn about their heritage. They did not speak Moroccan. They had gone to French schools and now English. Soumiya took English classes at the University of Paris.

She said, "Can you imagine a French teacher speaking English?"

The pronunciation is somewhat different. They sound more British than American. This is where I came to the rescue. You might say I do a form of tutoring. I corrected her during conversations. Understanding some words presented a problem. I would ask her to repeat the words, and then spell them. If that didn't work, I would look in the French-English dictionary. She had attended ESL (English as a second language) classes, and taken the GED test which she passed before they returned. At some future date, she planned to take classes at a college in the US.

I would help the sixth grader with homework. Once a problem was explained she could solve it. Those problems with several sentences in a paragraph were the worst. One day, I was trying to figure out what she didn't understand. The troublesome word was *coin*. After several tries, I got my change purse and dropped some coins on the table. That did it! The light came on.

Numerous papers were sent home from school. With three kids attending, it added to the confusion. I explained them all and Soumiya filled in the necessary blanks on those that had to be returned. You may wonder why they chose the Columbus area. Soumiya had family living in this area. Her brother owned the house they were occupying and was vacant at the time Mr. B's tour of duty ended in Paris. There are other brothers with families. There was also a possibility that the next assignment would be in the US possibly in Washington DC.

Shopping and looking for bargains was a favorite recreation. With three kids, there were a lot of needs. Soumiya is a beautiful woman and appearance is important. Having lived in Paris, she's familiar with brand names and the latest trends. Quality is something she is very aware of. Often, an item has to be returned. Some clerks have no patience with people who don't pronounce words exactly right at the refund counter. I would take over and it would be satisfactorily handled.

Other adventures have involved dental and eye appointments. I went along for support. Usually, I made the appointments. I've found that the biggest nightmare for immigrants was making business calls.

Many places use messages instead of humans for communicating. As a rule, these are spoken so fast that the caller cannot follow the information. I am not fond of this procedure but I can cope with it. I relayed the information and another problem had been solved.

Transferring the car title and getting a driver's license was an enormous undertaking.

It took several trips to the bank and the licensing agency. Soumiya had tried it on her own, but the clerk told her she hadn't been in the country long enough. We knew that information was incorrect. She had already passed the driver's test, now she needed her license. We stood in line waiting our turn, and would you believe, we got the same clerk and it was taken care of with no questions.

Soumiya is such a gracious person. She was always thanking me for every little thing. She wanted me to visit her the next spring in Morocco. Her home is not far from the beach and there are palm trees like in Florida. Helping her had been an adventure that I will always treasure. I missed them when they left. Though I had been to Morocco on a tour, I looked forward to visiting her family. Since then I have had the pleasure of visiting her twice. Her family showed me such a good time.

16   The Scorpion

Mike Harden, a columnist for the Columbus Dispatch, took a trip on Route 66 all the way to the west coast. He wrote about the places he stopped and picked up tacky souvenirs.

He asked his readers to write about which one they wanted and explain why. The only one I wanted was a small Lucite-encased scorpion paperweight. In his column in June 2003, he mentioned the winning letters and names along with their reasons. I got the scorpion. I wrote the following:

Dear Mike,

I am avidly following your column on the trip over Route 66 for sentimental reasons. In 1946, my husband and I traveled the same route in a brand new red Hudson convertible. We had been on a waiting list for a new car after the war. After my husband died, I served in the Peace Corps in both the Philippines and Costa Rica. My most frequent visitors

in my cement blockhouse in Costa Rica were
scorpions, which skittered across the floor
where I lived. I would like to have the souvenir
scorpion as a reminder of those days. Thank
You.

About a month later, I received the paperweight
in the mail. I love it!

17   The Later Years

Having an intermittent part-time job is comforting as prices of food and gas keep increasing. I don't travel as extensively since I have been on all the continents. Also, my traveling partner, Peg, no longer travels and other friends have passed on. I got a new Toyota, my third one since 1983. I drive to Florida where I own a mobile home at Hillcrest Community in Clearwater. All residents there are over 50.

Last year, my grandson, Jason, and I traveled to Saudi-Arabia. My son was in Bahrain on a job assignment. We had a great time. We went sightseeing all over and ate out everywhere. Don cooked one meal while we were visiting. We went to his office and met some of the locals. They treated me with such reverence as old age is respected overseas, very different than the US.

On the way to Florida in March, I visited my friend, Helen Murray, in Kingston, Tennessee. We drove to Oak Ridge and toured the area where the atomic bomb was built. There were busloads of tourists from everywhere at the museum.

In September of 1942, the government bought 59,000 acres in the mountains and 3000 residents were evacuated. They were told, "The Government needs your land to win the war."

In 1945, the population was 75,000. There were 10,000 family units, 13,000 dormitory spaces, 5,000 trailers, 16,000 barracks and a shopping center. With strict security, even children were required to wear ID badges.

Three plants were built. They worked around the clock. Peak employment was 130,000. No one was permitted to talk about their jobs. They were working to win the war. Scientists and other qualified personnel came from all over the country. Helen's husband was just out of high school and was hired. After Japan surrendered, the employees were told that they had built the bomb that ended the war.

Helen's daughter lives in Crossville, Tennessee in a home built in 1934, in Cumberland State Park, one of 250 houses in the Homestead Project. Linda and her husband lived in #24. Eleanor Roosevelt gave a speech where the first house would be built. Today 125 houses are still standing. Some were destroyed in fires due to faulty wiring. They did not at the time have electricity.

In 1934, the government bought 3000 acres to give to people to build homes. Singles got five acres, couples got ten and those with children got fifteen acres. All materials used were to be from their properties. Trees were cut down and rocks dug to be used for building. To this day, it is a beautiful area.

A few days later, I was on my way. There were many detours because of all the construction, part of the government programs putting people back to work. Unemployment was high, not quite as bad as during the depression in the 30s. This one was called the "recession."

During 2007, I had cataract surgery on both eyes. I now only wear glasses for small print or distance. The following year, I fell and broke my wrist. I had to wear a cast for six weeks. While I was in the hospital, they put me through a series of tests. I was sent to several doctors. I was given prescriptions, which created problems. I had bad reactions to Actonel and Prilosec. I became weak, anemic, no appetite, no energy—just to name a few issues. It took a whole year to get back to normal. Of course, I quit taking all of the medication. Later, when I had carpal tunnel surgery, I took no pills and had a good recovery.

When I was in Florida in 2009, my knee was hurting. My daughter, Joyce, had stem cell treatments successfully a few years before in

Miami Beach. I made the appointment with the doctor and we drove down. I had x-rays and my left knee had no cartilage left—it was bone on bone. I took the stem cell injections two days apart and within three days was walking. The cartilage slowly grew back. I took supplements and wore a knee brace for a few months. I did exercises every morning and followed the instructions I was given. I did everything slowly and by the end of the year I could do everything I wanted to do, including dancing. This eliminated the need for a knee replacement, at a cost of just under $3,000 on my credit card. My health insurance refused to pay a cent. After several tries, I gave up trying to collect.

I have gone to senior centers all over town since I retired. My favorite activity is line dancing, as you don't need a partner. The instructors have beginner's classes. My favorite one is in Grandview. Mary does an excellent job teaching the groups. Some of them perform for special occasions at fairs and different places. My exercise classes are also people over 55 at the Department of Defense, where I worked before my retirement.

18   Never Stop Working

When my house was sold in Bexley causing my rent to triple, I had to find a job. The senior employment agency sent me out to the Department of Agriculture. I took a test and was immediately hired at $7.50 an hour, in the spring of 2000. It was intermittent part-time work, as an enumerator. I worked four or five hours in the evenings and occasionally a half-day on Saturday. I called farmers and input information into the computer about crops, livestock, and acreage as well as related questions depending on whatever project we were calling about. My office is at the Department of Agriculture, but my employer is National Agriculture Statistics Service.

A few years later, I started working mornings from 7:30 a.m. until 1:00 p.m. or later. There have been a series of raises and am now earning $13.65 an hour. I enjoy this job, as it is also somewhat of a social thing. We can take time off for vacations or anything of importance as sometimes there are weeks with no projects to call about. Farmers are busier during the summer months. During these times, I will go two or three weeks with no work. I look forward to this time, so I can do other things. I have refinanced my house and reduced my payments. I no longer require this income to make ends meet, since I get increases in my retirement checks annually.

Some of the farms I call on have interesting names such as: Bacon Acres Inc., Aggravation Plantation, Agony Acres Farm, The Howard Animal Kingdom, and Campbell's Ewesful Acres.

Some answers to the questions are amusing like:

"I have eight acres."

"You call me a farmer?"

And the answer to the question of how many cows were milked yesterday, is: "All of them."

Of the messages on answering machines some are a diversion from statistics. This is a sampling of phone messages:

"I'm watching the millionaire program, can't talk and that's my final answer."

"Will call as soon as the cows come home."

"If you're a telemarketer, don't leave a message. Leave your name, rank and serial number and if I feel like it, I'll get back to you."

"You have reached the James Gang, and we're out robbing a train...leave your message."

"You have reached the number you dialed, amazing isn't it! What will they think of next?"

"Hello! Ha! You didn't really think I'd be sitting at the machine, did you?"

Conversations with a wife vary such as:
Q: "Have you seen the yellow questionnaire we mailed out?"
A: "I don't touch his mail."

Q: "Are you familiar with the cows?"
A: "I know they're black and white."

Q: "Are you familiar with the milk production?"
A: "Only the money, the bottom line."

Q: "Do you know about the cows?"
A: "No, Randy's the professional."

Q: "Is this a partnership?"
A: "I'm the unpaid partner."

Then, there are other comments:
"These guys complaining about the stock market, they ought to try farming."
"The price of wool is so low, we're using it for insulation in the shed to fill in the cracks."
"I was an engineer making $75,000 a year. I retired early to become a gentleman farmer. Last year, I figured my time and I made three cents an hour."

In addition to computer use on the job, I now have Internet at home and have learned to send e-mails. I may eventually get around to surfing the net. However, I'm old-fashioned and really prefer to talk to people on the phone or face to face.

Final Tidbits

Through the years, I have read all of Norman Vincent Peale's books on the "Power of Positive Thinking." I try to live by his words. They really help. I go to garage sales and when I find one of his books, I always buy it to give to someone I know who needs to change from negative to positive thinking. I am a great believer in positive thinking. I read the first book he wrote in 1948 on the subject. I still read many of his books, although he is no longer with us.

For years, I avoided the computer. The kids and grandchildren all said I should learn to use it. I was not interested, didn't want one. Then one day, Joyce gave me hers; she got a new one. Although I was reluctant, I started taking a class here and there. At the library, I eventually learned the basics. I like to play some of the games; my favorite is "free cell." I also have e-mail. My goal is to keep my mind active and learn new things. I watch a little television, but mostly prefer to read.

Not being domestic keeps me finding other things to do. I have no physical ailments, however a lot of my friends do. I take no medications. For me, the answer is proper nutrition and exercise. I do my own cooking and baking and rarely buy prepared meals.

Growing up during the Great Depression was a similar experience for everyone in the neighborhood. We were all in the same boat. We had food and shelter, love and friends. Clothing was passed around and everybody walked. Through the years I raised a family and had financial setbacks, but never gave in to them. I looked upon them as challenges. There was always a solution.

I've traveled in Europe several times, also in Canada. I've been in most of the 50 states and to Alaska and Hawaii more than once. I've crossed the equator on two different continents. In 1995, when Peg and I went to the Galapagos Islands in South America, we stopped at the equator in Ecuador before sailing down the Amazon River. In 2002 while on a safari in Africa, I stood on the equator in Kenya. I have framed certifications of these events.

The trip to India in 1996 was an eye opener, seeing the vast difference between the haves and have-nots. Along the highways are families living in makeshift tents begging, while the elite live in homes that look like palaces. Cows are sacred and they roam around on the roads. They have the right of way.

I was in London when Princess Diana died in 1997. My hotel was near her home where people lined up to pay respect to her. Flowers were everywhere and the guards were on white horses patrolling the area. Three days later, I watched the funeral on TV at home.

My friend of many years, Betty Hack, was
born in St. Gallen, Switzerland. Outside the
railroad station, stands a statue that Betty
posed for. Her neighbor was a sculptor and had
created a miniature statue before he sculpted
the life-sized one. I had always wanted to see
it. In 1998 while in Italy, I took the train to
St. Gallen and saw the statue. Betty died in
2005 at the age of 98.

During a trip to Vietnam in July 2007, I
toured the areas where our men had fought.
One interesting boat tour was down the river
to the bee farm where we had lunch. I took
a wagon ride around the area and stopped to
walk around. There were geese and various
animals. Our guide picked up a large python
and put it around his shoulders. He asked if any
one wanted to try it. I jumped at the chance.
I was so excited. My adrenaline was running.
I was amazed at how well it went. One more
adventure!

At the present time, I have no extensive travel plans. I'll go to Florida for a few weeks in the winter. I don't travel abroad as much since I have been on all the continents. During my career years I always made it a point to schedule vacations in the winter months. I'm still doing it. When my friends ask me which was my best trip, it's always hard to say, as each one had its highlights. In 2004, I had accomplished my goal. I had been on all the continents. I continually seek new avenues to explore.

As I finish my autobiography, I look forward to what lies ahead. When I had my palm read in India, I was told I would live past 100. Why not? I can compare myself to an older car, keeping up the maintenance, getting repairs and moving on.

Until the next trip...Adios!!!

Helen Reed...

...was born with lots of energy, courage and perseverance growing up with her Hungarian family in Ohio. Being a single mother of three back in the 40s proved her tenacity and bravery. She made an impact on the world through the Peace Corps and went on to travel the world. Today Helen continues to be healthy, happy and full of energy.

Snake...

...represents profound change and comes into our lives during the process of deep transformation, perhaps when we are struggling to let go of our former self. Awakening our intuitive energy, Snake guides us into the powerful and mysterious depths of our body, mind and soul. Holding our focus with Snake's unblinking stare, we gaze into eternity and emerge whole. This is where we birth our untapped power and creative wisdom.

CPSIA information can be obtained at www.ICGtesting.com
Printed in the USA
LVOW071413301111

257195LV00001B/73/P